Awkward Moments

DURING CHEAP HAIRCUTS

by Bill Paterson

PizzaDog
Studios

© 2016 Bill Paterson
Illustrations and design: Megan Sweeney
Design: Kathy Kastan
Library of Congress Cataloging-in-Publication Data:
Paterson, Bill
11 Awkward Moments During Cheap Haircuts / Bill Paterson
38p. 5 x 8 in.
ISBN 978-0-692-80952-5
1. Humor
10 9 8 7 6 5 4 3 2 1

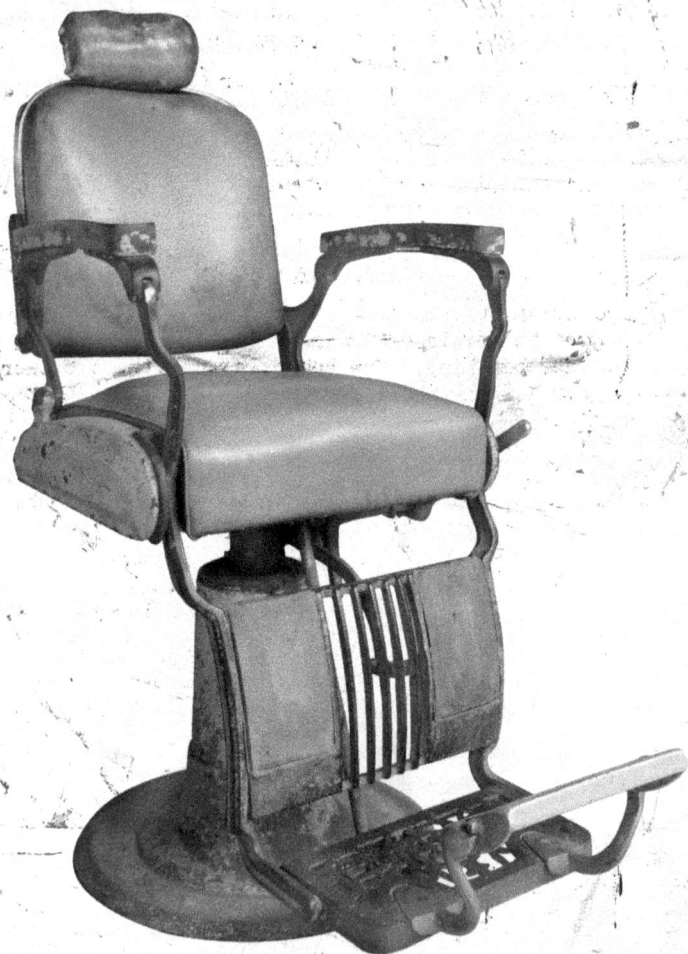

It'll Grow Back
(My Hair, Not My Dignity)

I refuse to allocate anything beyond $12 to the maintenance of my mane. See, I rock a pretty authentic homeless look. Investing in it would be akin to hiring a luxury landscaper to spruce up an abandoned textile mill.

No, I prefer to seek out the most economical follicle removal specialists I can locate. It's worth mentioning that I don't embrace this sad level of thriftiness in other aspects of life. My daughter doesn't subsist on discount cat treats and I don't engage in risky clinical trials to pay the cable bill.

There is a pitfall to this frugal philosophy, however. As you occupy that rejected dentist chair (wearing Batman's cape backwards), you are one vulnerable bastard.

Here are a few of the rabid-raccoon-crazy incidents that have befallen me inside this literal and figurative buzz saw.

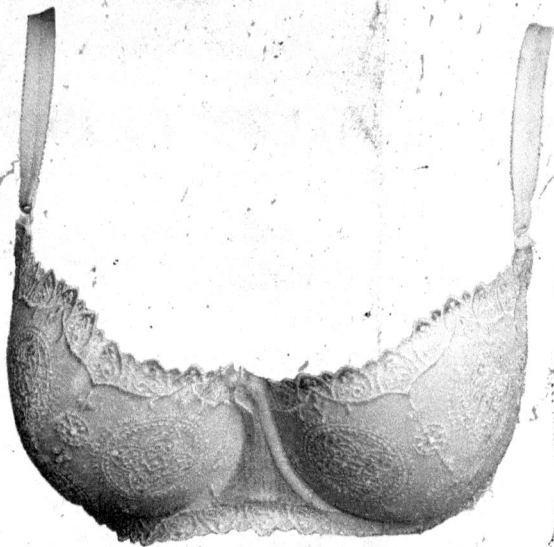

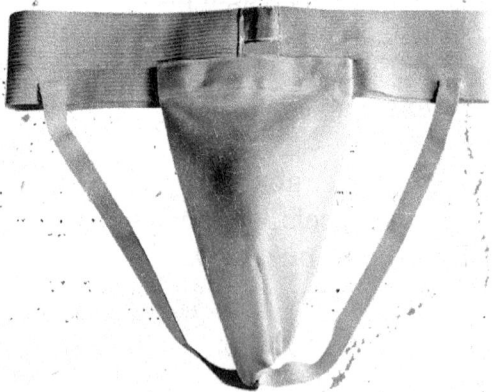

Hahaha...Sorry, Man

I witnessed the red-bespectacled lass
at the front desk appraise a customer
who, granted, was nondescript. Nonetheless,
this human was obviously capable of
producing a spermatozoon. No matter.
Our hostess coolly and calmly obliterated
the man's goddamned world.

"Name?"

"Allen."

"Helen?"

"Allen."

"Okay, Helen, it'll be about ten minutes."

That kill shot staggered Helen badly.
He just shambled on jelly legs to a plastic
chair, suddenly the owner of a new first
name and involuntary gender reassignment.

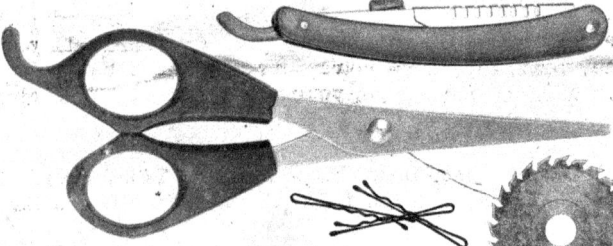

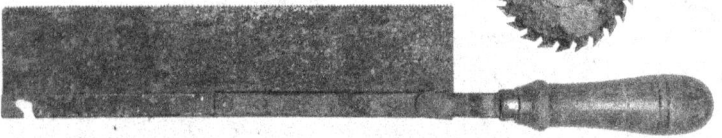

The Prison Headmistress

Once I was served (or, more accurately,
feloniously assaulted) by a matronly member
of the SWAT team.

Her touch was so impossibly vigorous, I was
holding back man-tears during the ordeal.

It felt like she was extracting each hair
individually with needle nose pliers.

I'm convinced she was purposely jabbing
me with her pot roast of a forearm to keep
me honest.

When she exploded in my ear with the
voice of Thor to say:

"SORRY, I THINK I CLIPPED YOUR EAR,"
everything went dark for a few moments.

Lady Fingas

○ ✂   ○ 💎   ○ 🛼

HEAD HUN-
TRESS

○ ✂   ○ 💎   ○ 🛼

2 Dye 4

Lil' Off

deepcutz

Sheering & Over-Sharing

I could pen volumes on TMI, a hallmark
of those who style dude-fur in exchange
for ducats. But here's one that begs for a
full transcript:

Hairdoer: (Asking mandatory opening
question): Big plans for the weekend?

Victim (Me): Yard work. Family stuff.
Probably dance like no one is watching.

**Hairdoer (Blowing right past the
dancing thing):** Good for you getting your
yard work done. I'm so jealous. My husband
hasn't touched our yard in months. He does
auto bodywork, 16 hours a day. Kids hardly
know who he is. Never touches ME either.

(Pause awkward enough to count
as two-and-a-half pauses)

Victim: If it makes you feel better,
I'm not seeding a cattle ranch or anything,
just moving a few leaves around.

Hairdoer: Oh, that's more than I can say
for him. He's making less money than his
old job paid too. Can you believe that?

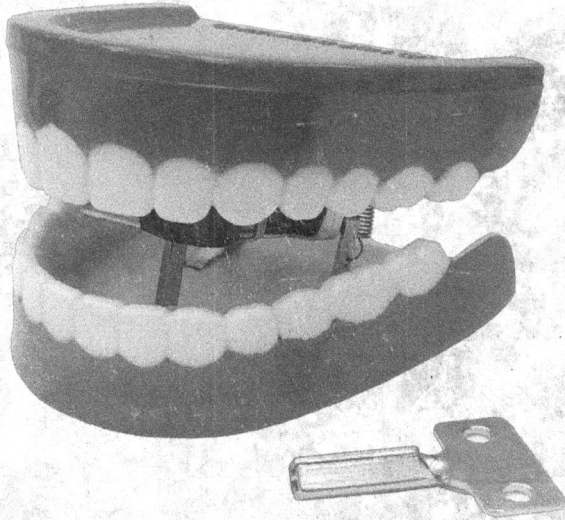

Victim: Wow that's…

Hairdoer: Yeah, $1,500 a month less.
You know what that means? Extra shifts for
me. I sooo don't want to be here right now.

**Victim (Said internally due to
cowardice):** Mother of sweet hell, please
don't gouge my cerebellum.

Hairdoer: But that's what I get for marrying
a guy for the sex. He just does it for me.

(417 awkward pauses)

Victim: I….could you thin it out on top a little?

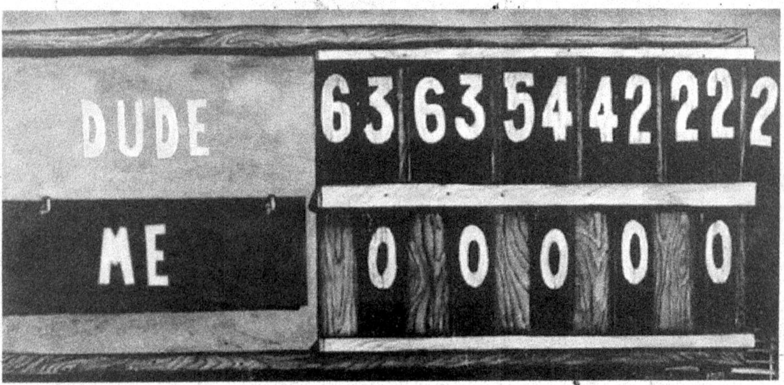
DUDE
6 3 6 3 5 4 4 2 2 2 2
ME
0 0 0 0 0

Dude, That's a Dude

This shit was inevitable.

Procure 12-15 haircuts yearly over a few
decades and one day you will find yourself
looking at two Adam's Apples in that mirror.
I handled it super well, too.

Because a gentleman who's styling hair
and wearing a t-shirt designed for a brassy
female toddler in all likelihood doesn't want
to talk sports.

When this fact became apparent, I panicked.
Like a jack-wagon, I just kept peppering that
poor sprite with all manner of references to
the day's impending football game.

Oh, we'll see who makes whom
uncomfortable today, Antonio.

Total She-Clipz

○   ○   ○

IVANA SNIPPIT

○   ○   ○

Sharp-Edgez

Unda Cutta

Ms. Tanglez

Jigsaw Is Displeased

To my immediate left was perched a
belligerent slab of Naugahyde blessed
with the voice of the villain from Saw.

The 4.7-minute wait time had exceeded
his acceptable threshold. How did
this malevolent soul choose to express
his discontent?

By machine-gunning Tuberculosis-
laden yawps of "C'mmmoonnnn!"
every 17 seconds. To their credit, the
scissor sisters clung to their standard
singsong of, "Be with ya shortly, hon!"

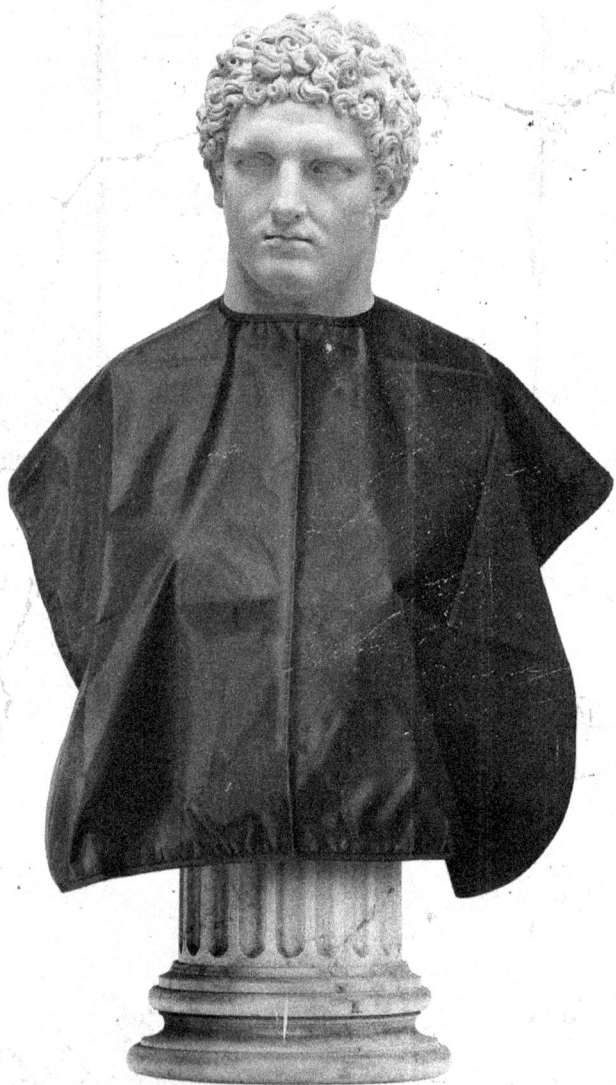

Just a Piece of Clay

A standard bargain-basement coif session
will require maybe 10-15 minutes of time
away from ESPN. Not this dark day.

The Michelangelo (Angela?) of stylists
clocked in at 26 minutes as she
sculpted me like a fucking hedge at
Buckingham Palace.

I used the time wisely, though.
I managed to dig out my phone
and learned a cool word for "hairy:"

Hirsute.

I'll use it in a sentence: That old goat in
the locker room indiscriminately flopping
his peen around is quite hirsute.

SHEAR TARA

○ ✂   ○ ◇   ○ 🛼

MANE -E- YAK

○ ✂   ○ ◇   ○ 🛼

Dread**Lox**

SHE BANGZ

'Do Me

Boob Action

This wasn't 14-year-old me rejoicing
that he has accidentally and fortuitously
touched a lady teat.

This was sort-of-adult me sucking my
ribs into my pancreas to avoid the
onslaught of boobage coming at me like
a pack of barely tethered hyenas.

Lord knows how many ta-tas were inside
this clown car of a blouse.

I hadn't felt such public indignity since
my purchase of a reversible men's belt
at Walgreens.

Educational Discourse

One very sweet cabeza-shaper surprisingly broached the divisive and nuanced topic of Common Core testing in elementary schools.

After I spewed some typical khaki-dad insights, she summed up her thoughts on the academic kerfuffle thusly:

"Those tests are just... re-donk-ulous."

Well, I suppose there's no counterpoint to that, Mindi with an "i." Now, about tending to this cowlick that makes me look like I was born to a woman who snorted bath salts.

Mrs. CleaveHer

○   ○   ○

$kizzor Sister

○   ○   ○

Blade Runna

Tressed Out

THE STILE

Nosy as Hell

There I sat.
Blood caked on the bridge of my snout.

Why?

Oh, because in the car, my iPhone flipped
out of my hand, did an impromptu triple lutz,
and careened into my unsuspecting sniffer.

Thanks to my normally sedate cellular device
having a grand mal seizure, I was left with a
seriously troubling facial disfigurement. One
that I then had to explain to a very chatty
chopper-chick.

I went with a cover story about taking a
racquetball to the face. I've never racquetted
a ball. But, I mean, just goddammit with this.

First Time, Long Time

It'd obviously been a while between rodeos
for Tammy, bless her spangly soul. She'd
raised some pups, spackled up her jaw-line
and jumped back into the styling game.

At first, I kinda dug her.

Mainly because she managed to use
the terms "crumb-bum" and "bargoon"
(the sassy way of saying "bargain").

Sadly, though, she shook off all those years
of rust right onto my cranium. Plus, she was
exhaling microns of menthol-light-infused
nicotine directly into my empty pores.

So I exited with a real shit-hack haircut –
and Emphysema.

THE MANE THING

○ ✂   ○ ♦   ○ 🛼

BUZZ-CUTTER

○ ✂   ○ ♦   ○ 🛼

SPITTIN' HAIRS

Wicked Chopz

THE BUTCH-HER

			REVISED 1008	TICKET NUMBER

☑ TR ☐ CM   **3**32302

	STATE	D.L TYPE
☐ D.L # ☐ COM DL # ☐ I.D #	▓▓▓▓▓	A B Ⓒ M

LAST NAME	FIRST NAME	MIDDLE INITIAL
▓▓▓▓▓	WILLIAM	▓▓▓▓▓

RESIDENCE ADDRESS	CITY
▓▓▓▓▓	BUFFALO

STATE	ZIP CODE	RES PHONE (AC)	DATE OF BIRTH
NY	▓▓▓▓	▓▓▓▓	▓▓▓▓

SOCIAL SECURITY NUMBER	WHITE BLACK HISPANIC ASIAN AMER. IND. OTHER	SEX M F	HEIGHT 5'10	EYES BL

EMPLOYER OR SCHOOL	BUSINESS ADDRESS	BUSINESS PHONE (AC)
▓▓▓▓	-	

OCCUPATION	SCHOOL ZONE? YES ☐	WORKER'S IN CONSTR. ZONE? YES ☐	HAZ MATERIAL? YES ☐	COMMERCIAL VEH? YES ☐

VEH. COLOR	VEH. YEAR	VEHICLE MAKE	BODY TYPE	REGISTRATION MONTH/YEAR	STATE	LICENSE PLATE #
BLK	2011	FORD	PK	05/16	NY	▓▓▓▓

VIOLATION DATE	VIOL. TIME	CONDITIONS:	NAME OF PARK OR SCHOOL
07/25/16	12 30 AM☐ PM☑	Day light Dark Dry Wet	-

VIOLATION LOCATION	COUNTY	DIRECTION
2459 NIA. FALLS BLVD.	NIA	NB

VIOLATION (A)	VIOL. CODE
DISOBEYING TRAFFIC CONTROL SIGN	

VIOLATION (B)	VIOL. CODE
BEING UNKEMPT	

VIOLATION (C)	VIOL. CODE

REASON FOR STOP

PS 3 _ _   VS 3 _ _   RFS 2   CAD # 901124834

Cell phone ☐	STEP ☐

ALLEGED SPEED: +3	SPEED LIMIT: 40	☐ RADAR ☐ LASER ☐ PACED ☐ AIRCRAFT ☑ VISUAL	COLLISION? YES ☑ BLUE FORM? ☐

OFFICER	EMP#	OFFICER	EMP#
▓▓▓▓		▓▓▓▓	

APPEARANCE DATE / FECHA PARA PRESENTARSE 09 - 13 - 16	READ CITATION FOR ADDITIONAL INFORMATION AND OPERATING HOURS

I HAVE RECEIVED THIS WRITTEN NOTICE TO APPEAR AND I WILL APPEAR AT THE CITY OF AUSTIN MUNICIPAL COURT ON OR BEFORE THE DATE AND TIME DESIGNATED ABOVE IN ORDER TO ENTER A PLEA OF GUILTY, NOT GUILTY OR NO CONTEST TO EACH VIOLATION LISTED ON THIS TICKET.

SU FIRMA ES LA PROMESA QUE SE PRESENTARA EN LA CORTE MUNICIPAL. PARA INFORMACIÓN LLAME A (512) 974-4890.

THIS IS NOT A PLEA OF GUILTY, ONLY A PROMISE TO APPEAR

DRIVER'S SIGNATURE/SU FIRMA
▓▓▓▓

READ INSTRUCTIONS ON THE BACK OF CITATION CAREFULLY

DEFENDANT COPY

Not Today, Jackass

Once, I actually failed to arrive at
the hair-removal outlet. Had a bit of a
cock-up on the road, which can be blamed
on the soulful strains of "Run-Around"
by Blues Traveler.

This corporate blues-rock classic mellowed
me out so much, I blew a red light and
smacked into some dullard. To be fair,
he was driving a real bag of belt buckles.

There was a witness to my brazen display
of vehicular negligence, which did not stop
me from throwing an indignant tirade
professing my innocence.

The officer of the law was unswayed,
but he made me feel like the only person
in the world as he wrote my summons.

CHEAP HAIRCUT PLACE	WHICH ONE IS IT? RAPPER	ROLLER DERBY CHICK

answers:

○   ○   ○

**So, two or three of these
are actual roller derby names.**

A couple are hair salons, maybe.

Some could be rappers for all I know.

**The point is, you had to
think about it for a second.**

**And that's why the
polar ice caps are melting.**